KONDWANI FIDEL

HUMMINGBIRDS IN THE TRENCHES

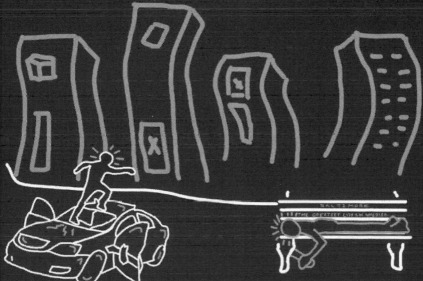

FOREWORD BY VALENCIA D. CLAY

ISBN-13: 978-1723519581
ISBN-10: 1723519588

Book Cover Art & Title Illustrations by Mikea Hugley.
@mikeahugley
www.cre8t1v3.com

Book production by Nikiea.

Author: Kondwani Fidel

Title: Hummingbirds in The Trenches

www.KondwaniFidel.com

To all of the Hummingbirds in the trenches, fly and fight your way to freedom. By any means necessary.

HUMMINGBIRDS IN THE TRENCHES
BY KONDWANI FIDEL

THE TRACKLIST

FOREWORD

you don't know what it's like to be a teacher in Baltimore or Harlem or any place that puts more money into juvenile jails than into our classrooms and have more hope for your boys than they have for themselves because what is hope in the middle of a blazing fire?

and you can always see the ashes in their eyes. and you can feel the soot on their fingertips.

to be a teacher that still has to teach even though you know your students are burning under the same sun that you stand in and youre sure they are learning while in your class despite their pain. you see the masks they wear and you reach underneath to pull out the innocence that fights for anyone to discover and stretch like a rainbow after the storm and you ask them what they want to be when they grow up and it's always something that makes money with no true joy or passion because eating is more important than creating and for that short year while they're in your class, you find the formula that it takes to tap into their tainted dreams, dreams that make their bones strong enough to show up to school as consistently as the day but it was already too late because before they met you their backs were branded by the system, the same system that employs you destroys them and you know this but you go to work to rewrite the story, this drowning narrative we are told is under our discretion and it is unless youre a little boy from a place that puts more money into your jail cot than into your neighborhood's library. you value what they teach us to teach you to value. and you learn from us, from them, that nothing is ever given to you unless you're locked with the promise of 3 meals a day. but when you're out here living free ain't nothing else free but your humanity, surely, is up for the taking. all cried out. a teacher that has to look at each of my boys tomorrow and read these articles about my former boys who will never be able to fly again and tell

them what is promised if they don't let me teach them now. tired.
tired of my babies being locked or killed or killing and maybe
this isn't the space for my rage but my therapy session isn't until
tomorrow evening, so I need to get this off my heart and make no
foolish inference that this is about me, it's about us. us. us. us. us.
us. us. us. us. us. us. us. us. us. us. us. u.

• • •

I wrote this over a year ago, but less than 5 days ago, another
one of my boys was murdered. Davon Davis. He used call me
ma' instead of Ms. Clay. Even the other teachers knew, I loved
him like he was my son. In the same way it is well known that
I love Kondwani, like he's my brother... because we share a
connection we never asked for: children who were neglected.
Davon's father and Kondwani's father are currently in the same
place. Their mother's share a similar plight, as well. Both raised
by their grandmothers. Is it a coincidence that both of them
are from East Baltimore? Is that even a question? Absolutely,
yes, and Hummingbirds in the Trenches amplifies the nuanced
answers.

The question is not raised as a reminder of why "this work
is important." We are already bombarded with viral videos of
brutalized, dehumanized, and demonized Black men, women,
and children on an unrelenting basis. Billie Holiday sang
about the bodies hanging from poplar trees. As a by-factor, she
spiraled into a deep depression, escaping her pain using heroine.
Social media would like us to believe that our generation is as
aware and affected by the blood on the leaves as she, but those
algorithms look differently on cell phone screens in the hood.
There is no action where there is a lack of education. And to not
know is to not do.

Why does the violence pop more than the conscious? Is is too much to face without losing oneself or are we desensitized? Those that do take a stance find themselves left to hang, as the very foundation of the field they spoke from is yanked from under them. Take Colin Kaepernick: for all 1,696 players in the NFL, they only needed to fire one to make an example of their ability to silence us.

Black pride remains a coping mechanism that soothes us sain, while the puppeteers of mass media sell the root of our anger as headlines and trending topics. They use our icons to fool us. Kendrick Lamar on the Grammy's. Beyoncé on a cop car. Big names with facades for influence where it is needed most. Because as much as the music knocks, and their messages are clear, where is the change?

Who is on the block, where little girls are asking "What the f*ck is Black girl magic?" Who is in the schools giving boys books that actually make them want to read? Those of us that still have a traumatized little boy or girl, looking for answers, direction, and love, living deeply within us. Kondwani is one of us and he is not simply writing from these trenches, he is healing them.

None of the work he is doing as a literary activist is for him, it's for those the work has yet to free.

Valencia D. Clay
Summer 2018

"An artist must be free to choose what he does, certainly, but he must also never be afraid to do what he must choose…We younger Negro artists who create now intend to express our individual dark-skinned selves without fear or shame. If white people are pleased we are glad. If they are not, it doesn't matter. We know we are beautiful. And ugly too. The tom-tom cries and the tom-tom laughs. If colored people are pleased we are glad. If they are not, their displeasure doesn't matter either. We build our temples for tomorrow, strong as we know how, and we stand on top of the mountain, free within ourselves."

— *Langston Hughes*

"There's all sorts of trauma from drama, that children see
Type of shit that normally would call for therapy
But you know just how it go in our community
Keep that shit inside, it don't matter how hard it be
Fast forward them kids is grown and they blowin trees."

— *J. Cole.*

"If you don't tell your story, you're giving society the space to kill you."

— *D. Watkins.*

THE PRELUDE

A few summers ago I was walking up Monument Street in 98-degree weather, shirtless, heading to North East Market which is the only semi-fresh-food hub in my neighborhood. I ran into my childhood friend Chris and he said, "Yo, I never knew you had that scar on your stomach. What happened?" I told him that I was diagnosed with Pylorics Stenosis as an infant and had to undergo a death-biting surgery to keep me alive, which left a permanent gash right above my belly button and another two on my right and lower abdomen. Chris's rebuttal was, "That's crazy. I'm surprised you ain't die. You know Johns Hopkins be killing Black people." I didn't know what he meant, but that became a mundane phase that I heard then on out from people in my community. This made me recall the time my mother told me a story about how, after my surgery, the Johns Hopkins Hospital (JHH) workers declared me dead, which ended up being a "mistake," after they saw how berzerk my mother went.

I wanted to find out more information regarding this alleged Black blood that JHH has had on its hands. I then started to conduct some research and glued my eyes to texts, such as Medical Apartheid by Harriet Washington; the JHH workers trying to kill me was no longer a mystery.

I read through the dark and disgusting studies of unethical medical experimentations on Black Americans from colonial times to the present. I discovered that in the mid- 1900s, Baltimore's Kennedy Krieger Institute (KKI), an institute affiliated with Johns Hopkins Hospital, held a "Lead-Based Paint Abatement and Repair and Maintenance Study." This study kept or placed Black families who had small children in ramshackle homes, knowingly exposing them to dangerous levels of lead. If lead paint was a basketball player, it would be a hall-of-famer for causing severe illness and chronic mental retardation in young Black children who inhale airborne lead dust and swallow the paint chips like their favorite UTZ. KKI carried out their agenda by working with landlords to lure Black families into these lead-tainted homes with food stamps, money, toys, and other necessities a poor family might need. This study was allegedly carried out to eliminate future lead threats. "They monitored changes in the children's lead levels as well as the brain and developmental damage that resulted from different kinds of lead-abatement programs," according to Medical Apartheid. The parents were not informed that this study would be placing children at a high risk of lead exposure.

After several years of taking advantage of and decimating thousands of Black children with lead paint poisoning, on August 16, 2001, the courts ruled against this experiment, juxtaposing it to the Tuskegee Syphilis Experiment. Judge J. Cathell noted, "It can be argued that the researchers intended that the children be the canaries in the mine."

When I originally read Judge J. Cathell's phrase, "canaries in the mine," I didn't know what it meant, but a quick Google fix changed that. In the 20th century, miners would tote canaries with them into the tunnels when working. If dangerous gasses such as carbon monoxide were in the tunnels, it would kill the innocent canaries before killing the flesh-peddling miners, providing them with a clear cut warning to immediately evacuate the tunnels or put on protective respirator gear.

I said to myself, "Damn, that's really messed up, canaries didn't deserve that." Canaries in the mine were guiltless creatures who were being murdered for research purposes, which was arguably to help build a better world. But some would say the sacrifice of canaries was in "God's plan," which doesn't make sense to me. But then again, the desire to oppress and murder the vulnerable has never been justified with logic here in America. The justification to oppress and murder has never been based on facts; instead, it is based on false beliefs.

Do you think that in God's little notepad, he wrote, "These canaries are meant to be captivated, held against their will and murdered?" or "After we release the shackles and chains from these Black folks, we're gonna create racist laws and policies to keep them padlocked to poverty, prison cells, and an unfair lifestyle while living in America?" Nah, I don't believe that.

Canaries were not born with the sole purpose of being prisoners of miners. The people in my community were not born with the sole purpose of being prisoners of the American streets that conceived them.

I call those modern day prisoners in my community "Hummingbirds in the trenches."

Hummingbirds in the trenches flutter in an ocean of smoke. While some Hummingbirds drown in this ocean, there are others who fly out to find dry land. Touching down on this dry land is the Hummingbird's attempt to flee its cage. If open-minded, the Hummingbird will become aware of a liquid light, which is the realization that he or she is a universal life force, which debunks the myth that the Hummingbird's "proper place" is that back door Carter G. Woodson mentioned in The Mis-Education of the Negro. After finding this liquid light on dry land, the Hummingbird attains a new way of thinking, which ultimately exposes the Hummingbird to a better lifestyle. If passed down, these newly- found ideas lead to resources that serve as opportunities for the other Hummingbirds who have not yet experienced this dry land and what it has to offer.

People constantly ask Hummingbirds like myself, "What makes you different than the others?" By "the others," they mean the ones who have not yet made it to this dry land. I frequently have to explain that there is no distinction between me and them. I am them and they are me. I just happened to stumble across some opportunities that aren't awarded to everyone in my community, and I made something out of them. All of the Hummingbirds in the trenches are born with a genius-level talent and a towering amount of love that almost always gets bulldozed by our environment which cages us.

When I was touring in the United Kingdom a few months ago, I realized how important my voice is. I was in a foreign country sharing my stories and the stories of other Hummingbirds--with not only the British, but people from all around the world. Humanizing the Hummingbirds for these strangers is one thing, but it doesn't compare to the hope I was able to give my fellow Hummingbirds when telling our stories abroad: like every other group of people, we have imperfections, but we are beautiful and benevolent. They try to kill us off, but Hummingbirds don't die, we multiply.

I've inspired people to become writers, poets, entrepreneurs, and just better versions of themselves. I've motivated a nation of Black and Brown little boys and girls throughout this world. My book Raw Wounds has been taught at universities across the country, and even the globe, including the University of East London. My work has also made it to public and private schools throughout the nation, such as City Springs Elementary/Middle School in East Baltimore and Brooks School in Massachusetts.

Hummingbirds in The Trenches is a glimpse of what's seen through my eyes, a touch of what I taste, a buzz of what I hear, and a whiff of what I smell. The complex idea of death has been ricocheting in my brain while writing this book, so it will be present when your eyeballs wander through the lines I've penned.

I've seen Hummingbirds aim their first gun at the mere age of 10. Not that they wanted to murder, they just didn't wanna "get caught slippin'." I once slept with pistols and drugs stashed in my bedroom ceiling: a double life sentence resting over my skull. Imagine sleeping with ghosts who crave power, with the sole purpose to control your spiritual.

We Hummingbirds didn't ask to have our freedom and God-given rights snatched from us. We didn't ask to receive brain damage from lead paint poisoning. We didn't ask for our schools to look like prisons. We didn't ask for our everyday to involve bullets, splattered brains, and bullshit. We didn't ask for America's inequitable policies to serve as a malignant cancer to the Black community. However, we still find the stamina to sing. We might not always sing what's comfortable for the sensitive ears; nonetheless, we sing what's on our hearts.

Hummingbirds in The Trenches is an assemblage of songs. Some may make you weep, and some may make you laugh. Some you may play on repeat, and some you may pass.

Welcome to the trenches.

A DEATH NOTE

If the sounds of gunshots were generated into song sales, Baltimore would've gone triple platinum by now. Murder has been opening its mouth like a hungry lion, eating away more than 220 lives in 2017, and it's only August. It was 3:00 a.m. and I was laying down on a pint-sized mattress in a cramped dorm room at the University of Illinois at Chicago. I had had a long day of writing workshops, so I decided to hit up the The Violet Hour, a bar in Wicker Park, where I guzzled four vodka gimlets to end my late-night/early-morning. I was plastered, numb to all misery, until my phone buzzed. I checked it, and an alert read, "Man killed in Greenmount Avenue shooting becomes city's 200th homicide victim." I stared at the ceiling as cold tears slid down my cheek, chilling the back of my neck. I started to reminisce about all of my family and friends who expired on the streets of Baltimore. Depression crept down on me, hope seemed futile, and I wanted to fade out like Robin Williams. I called on God, but his phone was on Do Not Disturb; it seems as though he always ignores me when I need him the most. Every time a body drops in my city, no matter if it's a loved one or not, a piece of my sanity is chipped away.

We live in a country that marks Black babies at a popular price of null and void. Since I was a small child, I've had family and friends murdered under these Baltimore skies, and it's been killing me, literally.

It was the summer of 2003 when bullets snatched all 26 years of Trav's life. Trav was my aunt Lisa's boyfriend, and my uncle Neil's best friend. Trav treated me like I was one of his own, and the love was mutual. I was 10 years old, and school had just ended for the year. I was chilling with Uncle Neil at his crib, waiting for him to get dressed, so we could go back around my way and meet up with Trav. I was awakened out of my sleep by a loud, "Nooooooo, not my nigga!" This would be an introduction to a phrase that inevitably became commonplace as I grew older. His shriek suppressed the lyrics of 50 Cent's "Get Rich or Die Tryin'" that was blasting through the speakers. I woke up and saw Uncle Neil pacing back and forth throughout the living room while veins bulged out of his sweaty forehead. I was afraid to ask what was wrong. But my childlike curiosity burned. "Unc, what happened?" A minute or two passed, and he sat on the couch beside me and cried. I didn't know what was going on, but I felt his pain, and I started to cry, too.

"They killed Trav," Uncle Neil said, as he struggled to get the three words out. This was also my introduction to "they." "They" is a person or persons that I would also hear stories about for a lifetime.

Uncle Neil and I walked on Hillen Road and flagged down a hack, and were driven to my house, two blocks over from where

Trav was murdered. When we arrived, the entire neighborhood was in shambles. I can't remember a soul who wasn't crying. For the next few weeks I witnessed how Trav's death tore Uncle Neil apart. The harsh smell of rotten teeth mixed with Steele Reserve 211 was rushing out of Uncle Neil's mouth every time he spoke. Liquor was his fling-turned-wife.

This is my earliest memory of being spiritually and emotionally connected to death in Baltimore, and also my first time seeing how it affected the people around me. However, this wasn't my last. My aunt Lisa, on the other hand, has had three of her significant others slaughtered in my city. Because her chin is always parked in the air, she doesn't ever show the slightest glimpse of grief, but I'm sure she's afflicted with pain.

My second encounter with death was later that same year of Trav's farewell. This time, it wasn't a close friend, and it wasn't murder. It was my seven-year-old little brother Fidel and his 11-year-old brother Davon. It was approximately 4:00 am when ambulances and fire trucks rushed the block. A firefighter pulled a limp salmon pink object from the hell-fire which ended up being Fidel. Some minutes later, they yanked out Davon.

The following day, I walked to Johns Hopkins Hospital to visit Fidel. At this point, Davon had already succumbed to his injuries and died in the hospital before I had chance to see him a final time. All of Fidel's hair, gone. His head was swollen. Blisters the size of boiled eggs covered his baby face. Large tubes took an excursion through his throat, nose, penis, and other body parts. I shook his body with my small palms, as I whispered, "Fidel...Fidel."

He didn't budge so I shook him a little harder and my voice got a little louder.

"FIDEL!…FIDEL!"

He didn't respond or budge.

Later the next day, I received a call from my grandmother. She said, "Fidel died…We had to pull the plug." I wasn't familiar with the word 'suicide,' but I knew that I didn't want to live any longer, and I was coming up with all sorts of ways to make that happen.

After Trav, Fidel, and Davon all died in such a short time, I knew for sure that I was gonna bite the dust soon.

***

Keon was 16 years old when a bullet struck his dome while standing on an East Baltimore corner in 2009. I was 16 at the time, too. Hours before his brains splattered on dirty marble steps, Keon rode through my block to holla at me.

"Yo, Ima bring some girls through the block later, they bad as shit."

"Bet, just hit my phone, I'll be around," I responded, as I gave him a fist-bump and watched him wheelie away on his silver Mongoose.

A few hours later, my homie Dre ran up Jefferson Street wearing a sweaty grey wife beater. In and out of deep breaths, Dre said, "Yo…Guess What?…Keon…Just got popped!" I dropped my iced tea, and my homies and I sprinted towards Linwood Avenue where Keon was hit. As soon as we arrived, the street was decorated with yellow tape, blue and red lights, and women in pj's, shaking their heads while tears drained from their ducts: a sight that became a day-to-day thing.

A white sheet covered a body, which I denied was Keon until I scanned the premises and saw his lone green 498 New Balance sneaker napping in the middle of the street. This was my first time seeing a visual representation of a popular phrase in conversation in my neighborhood, and in rap songs:"Blow a nigga out his shoes."

Where I come from, crying is a sign of weakness, so I routinely rubbed my eyes, making sure no tears fell.

Keon was gone, and all I kept asking myself was, "Will I be next?" To hide this pain, I was freakin-off with a massive amount of women, I was barely eating, I drank Four Loko long past after my kidney felt like it was gonna burst, and I smoked hella blunts. I had hopes of going to college, but I just knew that the streets would do me in before freshman orientation because everybody's melon was gettin' cracked. Death was all around me, and it didn't have an age limit or gender preference.

***

April 14th 2014, I was sitting in Gateway Hall, a dormitory at Virginia State University. Thanks to my ambition, and luck, I made it to college. I was working on promotion material for a collection of poems I was planning to release. I received a call from my little brother Antuane. "Yo, Shad got stabbed." Shad was my best friend. We shared clothes, shoes, and money. Shad's grandmother sold weed, but she always gave us dimes for free. One night she gave us something close to an ounce, and we shared it with these two sisters from our neighborhood and ended up bangin' them both on the same bed. Shad was a friend that I'd give my last. My last kidney, my last shot of yak, my last piece of chicken, you name it.

I instantly hung up the phone with Antuane and started praying. I got another call from him 10 minutes later and I heard him crying through the other end. I screamed, "Don't do this to me Tuane, why the fuck are you lying?" He continued to cry, then he said, "Shad is gone my nigga." I left out of the lounge area and started walking back to my room. My motor skills conked; you would've thought Mike Tyson punched me in the stomach the way I dropped to the floor. My tears flooded the floor, as people walked passed, looking at me as if I were crazy. At this point, I wouldn't have disagreed with them. I was broken.

I went home and found out that Shad got into an altercation with a guy at a gas station. A fight broke out and Shad got jabbed in his liver several times with a small sword. He crawled into his car and locked himself inside to escape the clutches of his newfound enemy. Shad's suede seats chugged liters of his blood, and he slithered into the opening arms of the grim reaper.

Ya'll know what I did for the next few months: gave no fucks, and went to class drunk damn near every day, as professors gave me side eyes. I know they smelled that sauce seeping through my pores.

Every day for the next few months, alcohol bit a hole in my pocket, and I routinely locked myself in my dorm room for many nights with 2 Pac's "Thugz Mansion" and Rihanna's "What's Love Without Tragedy?" on repeat, as I killed myself. They were the only two songs that could understand me. I got disconnected from many of my college friends because I inched further away from the guy they once knew.

I became careless and dispassionate when it came to school and relationships. I wanted to be by myself, and many people just couldn't understand. I thought that I was gonna drink myself into casket or die from stress before I even made it to senior year. I was ready for the ride.

***

D was 21 when he got splashed in West Baltimore. It was January, 2015.

I had just returned to my neighborhood after performing some spoken word poetry to a group of students. I was standing out front of JJ's carryout in East Baltimore, watching cars bounce down the lumpy roads of Monument Street as I waited for my chicken box. Fifteen minutes passed and I walked into the store to check on my food. "Ayyeee Mama! Those 4-wings-and-fries ready?" I said as I tossed my ticket into the circular plexiglass portal where money, food, and arguments about wrong orders get exchanged. I received my food, left JJ's, and stopped inside of Rod's Barbershop, which is a few stores down. As I gave dap to friends and associates, I received a call.

"Yo guess what?"

"What's good?"

"You heard D got murked last night?"

I hung up my phone in disbelief and shrieked, "Fuck!" while everyone stared. I left the barbershop and did what I do best to cope. I hit the bar and grabbed a pint of Absolut and a pack of Black & Milds, and started my healing ritual.

D, Shad, and I all hung in the same camp. Every time I looked at old pictures of me and my friends, I saw fewer people, and I couldn't help but to embrace an early death. I mean how could I not?

Suffering from the mental and emotional pain that stems from murder and violence is one of the many ways that Black people die in America. Every single day I ask, "Will the murder ever stop?" and the more I learn, I understand the hard truth, and the answer is, no. Aside from the names of the people I mentioned above that died, there are countless deaths that troubled me while living in Baltimore and being connected to her hip. I have stacks of obituaries, and I can't count how many funerals I attended.

A list of things I've seen at funerals: fist fights amongst friends, family, and I've even seen a pastor get knocked out by a quick jab. Drunken fathers have jumped in the ground screaming, "I want to be buried with my son," at burial sites. I even know of some people who committed suicide after losing a loved one. When anger has been bottled up for ages, anything is liable to take place.

I can't count how many shoulders I cried on, nor the amount of people I lent shoulders to.

Everyone in my city knows someone who's been murdered. Thousands of people are suffering from some type of mental anarchy that stems from violence. As I started to do research on violence and murder, the tragedies in Baltimore started to make sense.

***

I stumbled across an article in Bloomberg that said, "Baltimore is the worst place in America to grow up poor and male." I know that my city is extremely difficult to survive in, but I never knew that it was the worst in the country. I did more scholarly lurking, and discovered that, Harvard economists Raj Chetty and Nathaniel Hendren researched a child's chances of future success by collecting a list of the 100 largest counties in America.

The two economists studies show that "Baltimore is at the bottom. But It's really at the bottom for boys." This is a result of what I call "zip code genocide."

Baltimore is a city where "everyone knows each other." This city has roughly 620,000 residents, and 63% of those people are Black. The Black people stay and hang out where they live, and vice versa for white people. Baltimore has two identities, and depending on where you reside, depends on what you call it. My friends and I call it 'Bodymore Murderland.' The white people call it 'Charm City.' We eat chicken boxes and other phony foods while standing on small blocks-adjacent to dice games-under blue lights, and we converse about who got murdered the night before, the new chicks who moved in the hood, who got beat up by the cops that day. We drink cheap vodka that burns our chest, and temporarily scraps our heartache.

White people walk their expensive dogs, do yoga, have avocado food fights in Whole Foods, and drink Non-GMO-Gluten-Free Pinot Grigio, I think. Nonetheless, there are two Baltimores, and your zip code determines whether or not you live or die. Poor and concentrated poverty communities have lower employment, lower educational attainments, higher crime, and poorer health outcomes than other areas. The History, Public

Policy, and the Geography of Poverty data reveals, "About 80% of Baltimore City's poor live in a poverty area, whereas across the rest of the State, 17% of the poor live in a poverty area."

Poverty is a modern day slave-ship with a little more leg room.

Poverty imprints barriers that deny Black people the opportunity to achieve promising education, well-paying jobs, and sanity, which leads to murder, depression, and suicide. Suicide doesn't always come with a rope, pistols, or prescription pills. In poor living circumstances, suicide is masked-up in drug addiction, self-doubt, murder, and other things, which stifles Black progression and strengthen Black people's despair.

The large majority of Americans expect Black people to "pull themselves up by the bootstraps," and become "better people," and that will amend poor Black people's economic status, the racial disparities, and the racial discrimination they face. Placing these incriminations on Black people and not the systems that enslave, murder, and oppress Black people, is criminal. It is also one of the many racist ideas that keep Black people chained to an inferior status in this society.

***

Poverty will remain undefeated, squeezing people into emergency rooms and graveyards. By the end of this year, if this pace continues, the death rate will be swollen like broken jaw bones, making 2017 the deadliest year ever in Baltimore. Grandmothers will outlive their grandkids and the smell of sizzling flesh will dangle over nappy fades and colorful barrettes.

However, I'm supposed to pretend that I'm happy, while I walk on ground where shy blades of grass grow plump from swallowing the blood of babies.

I'm supposed to pretend that I'm happy, while I wait on bus stop corners where deflated balloons choke dirty light poles, and hard melted candle wax covers marble steps; the cries of mothers attending vigils ricocheting on my ear drums.

I'm supposed to pretend that I'm happy, although a million screams from absent sons and daughters ride my brain eternally. I'm supposed to pretend that I'm happy, while envisioning the faces of the crying children that killed you: the ones who pop pistols shed tears, too.

I'm supposed to pretend that I'm happy, knowing that death has said its farewell to "around the corner," and is now dancing at my peephole. I'm supposed to pretend that I'm happy, knowing that many parents don't have a fair chance at raising their children productively in this smoky city.

I'm supposed to pretend that our zip codes don't determine whether or not we live or die? I'm supposed to pretend that zip code genocide doesn't lead to depression, suicide, and homicide? Nevertheless, I don't have any more patience in me to be fake-happy. I'm aching, my sanity has been shattered, and I don't mind accompanying the rest of them in paradise, if there is one.

This isn't a sob story, just my self-expression. I don't want you to "feel me," because 9 times outta 10, you won't be able to do so anyway. Your harm reduction strategies won't work around here because this is a no-heal zone. There are more than 16,000 ran down vacant homes in my city, and we lose loved ones to murder and drug overdoses every day. Where I live, there are no "safe spaces." Where I live, yoga can't stop bullets from piercing through the livers of my homies. As long as there is poverty, there will be murder, and where I live, blood will continue to shed.

I don't have a one-sized-fits-all solution to these problems. I do believe that as a people, we need to get the ones who don't understand the importance of literacy on board. This will lead to critical thinking, which leads to effective decision making; I believe in that, lies hope. Being devoted to changing the world using art is hard for anyone, especially a twenty-four-year-old like myself. Just like SZA, "I'm prayin that my 20-somethings don't kill me."

Rest in peace to all of the children who were born—a bullet wound, a bad day, a bloody skull, a body bag.

As long as guns thunderclap, striking holes through flesh; so long live the lost Black angels, and the ones who are next. I hope that this song serenades forever.

THEM

This is for them boys and girls who get jailed
by schools and schooled by jails
Growing up a block away from Hell
A short stone's throw from

This for them boys and girls who step
foot in the church only for funerals
No bible study on Wednesday's
Gotta get them packs off, rent paid

This is for them girls who march to grocery stores
in food deserts, leaving footprints of pain
Bonnets bop through the trenches

This is for them boys who can't sleep
til Mamma's company leaves
Couch = bed
Your back is touching your cousin's knees

This is for them girls who get cat-called
she reports, then gets Blackballed
due to her Black scars

This for them   boys and girls
Drag you when your brows ain't done
Society demonizes your make-up
Still beautiful

Unless we're shootin', no one notices the youth

My first piece of jewelry as a child was purchased at a pawn shop on the corner of Monument st. and Collington ave, a few blocks up from where I lived in East Baltimore. It was a gift from my granny. Oh, I could only imagine how many stories that lived on the mounting of that gold ring. The various faces it slapped. Or how many phat asses it grabbed. Or how many times it was handed over after a swift pistol whip. Or how many specs of blood spanked the diamonds during fistfights. Or how many cigarettes, Steele Reserves, and half-n-halfs it clutched like a new purse. Pawn shop jewelry has many stories untold, and I would share with you all some of my experiences with the ring, but that'll be no fun. So I'll let you imagine, just like I did.

Sometimes I Just Don't Wanna Be Here Anymore

A scarred brown palm flew in the air. A squeaky preteen voice followed. "Can you tell me how to cope with suicidal thoughts? Because sometimes I just don't wanna be here anymore."

I was sitting in front of a class of middle-schoolers who were reading my book Raw Wounds, when a student asked this haunting question. I can't lie, I asked the kids, "Do you have any questions before I start speaking?" I wrongfully assumed they would've raised questions about my book. Boy, was I wrong.

My tongue got replaced with a stone. My eyeballs bounced like fast dribbles. My throat got clogged—it felt like a gun was jammed in the back of my mouth. My mind scrambled like a quarterback in the pocket—it was fourth and long in the final quarter with seven seconds left on the clock, we were down by two points. I peeked through the bars on my face mask, head moving back and forth. I looked for an open receiver, BOOM! I'm sacked. I fumbled.

This wasn't the first time that a student asked me a question of this stature. However, because I didn't have a response, this particular altercation lit a fire inside of me.

Suicide is the sixteenth leading cause of death for Blacks of all ages, and the third leading cause of death for Black males between the ages of 15 and 24. After researching this information, I had a better understanding as to why children want to kill themselves. I live in a city where children eye-witness bullets zooming past their own earlobes—that same bullet then strikes the back of their friend's neck. I live in a city where grandparents bury their children and grandchildren regularly. I live in a city where lead paint poisoning and fentanyl are catching record-breaking bodies. I live in a city where your zip code determines whether or not you die. I live in city where kids have knocked on God's door, been ignored several times, then come to me asking about suicide. Many of these children can't picture better lives for themselves—some will never get close to nibbling a piece of that American pie—so that's why they crave to kill themselves.

Suicide Awareness Voices of Education studies show that seven in 100,000 youth ages 15 to 19 die by suicide each year, 12.7 in 100,000 young adults ages 20-24 die by suicide each year, male deaths represent 79% of all US suicides, and there is one death by suicide in the US every 12 minutes. There is so little conversation about so much blood shed.

I came across a headline the other day that said, "Family stunned by Boy's Suicide Attempt That Killed Driver." A 12-year-old boy belly-flopped from an overpass in Virginia and ended up landing on an SUV, killing a 22-year-old woman. I also found out that a 10-year-old boy stabbed himself in the chest, taking his own life in Memphis, Tennessee. These two incidents are deeply troubling; however, they are lint-ball-sized when you take a glimpse of the rate that young people are killing themselves.

In 2015, the Centers for Disease Control and Prevention discovered for the first time ever that "the suicide rate of Black children between the ages of 5 and 11 had doubled between 1993 and 2013…Suicides by hanging nearly tripled among Black boys in particular."

In impoverished communities similar to the one I am from and currently live in, suicide and depression are words that are always left out of conversation when speaking about the ways that Black people die. Being as though these acts of suicide regarding Black people are directly connected to poverty and poor race relations in America, there is not a universal solution to this issue. What I will say is that we need to start being more open about our feelings and emotions whole-heartedly so we can shift the culture and the way that we handle discussions around suicide and depression.

Quite often, my joy hops in a jet and deserts me, leaving me wounded while in the company of life's troubles. Being open about what's killing you can help save a life or two. That might not sound like a lot, but rescuing one is better than not rescuing at all.

BEING A GEMINI

Me: "Idk, I've just been feeling depressed lately."

Lor Q: "Oh you're good. That's just that Gemini sh*t"

Me: "I don't believe in horosc—"

Lor Q: "Bro, you're only emotional right now because the full moon is Gemini."

Me: "So what about the other times when the moon was't full?"

Lor Q: "Yo, you're thinking about it too much. You really being a Gemini right now."

OCTOBER 17, AT 3:48 PM IN PINE RIDGE, SOUTH DAKOTA

I remember sitting on the curb watching bugs, dead birds, soaked cigarette butts and empty potato chip bags slide down the infested waters like kids at Six Flags' water park—them gutters were a jungle. I use to dream that I could shrink myself and surf on those empty bags into the nearest sewer—I used to wanna be a Teenage Mutant Ninja Turtle.

Will God help the children?

It is HARD SLEEPING IN A CAGE

My heart was pounding like the paws of a panther chasing its prey—it was 5:33 in the morning. I kept waking up in 60 minute intervals. "Why the fuck can't I sleep?" seeped out of my crusty brown lips. I went to the kitchen to grab a bottle of water, but there weren't any left. I stuck my dome underneath the faucet, cranked the cold water, and heard my dehydrated insides throw a party. "Damn, I need to start drinking more water."

I went back into my room and sat on the end of my bed in silence while Big K.R.I.T.'s Drinking Sessions spilled through my mini speaker. After spinning the song a few times, I attempted to get some rest. As soon as I shut my eyes, my cousin's dog Summer, who lives right above me, squirmed in her cage. Her cage continuously rattled for roughly 35 minutes. Another 35 minutes that's thrown into my box of sleepless nights. The entire time I was cursing her out in my head: "I

hate this bitch. She always trippin when I'm trying to sleep."
"Why did my cousin even get a dumbass dog?" "I just wish that
she would shut the fuck up."

I ended up not going to sleep but taking a small nap until the
7:00 a.m. sun pierced my curtains. I woke up thinking about
Summer, wondering why is it that she makes the most noise
when it's bedtime. Then it hit me.

My sleepless nights lead to random walks throughout the
house, shutting doors, faucet turns, and tip-toeing on creaky
wooden floors. I'm pretty sure that this keeps Summer from
enjoying her sleep, just as much as she keeps my eyes wide
open during bedtime. I realized that Summer and I are both
pigeonholed to a prison.

My mind is caged by permanent paranoia. When will I
get popped by a killer cop and look down from the heaven
skies and watch my body lay lifeless? What family member
or friend will overdose on fentanyl today? Who's gonna jam
a pistol to the back of my head when I'm walking to Pizza
Boli's? When am I going to make enough money to move my
family out of the trenches? When will happiness be a day-to-
day feeling? When will I be able to substitute the noodles and
crackers with ribs and shrimps? Paranoia has me in a headlock.

Dear Summer, I too know that it is hard sleeping in a cage.

HOOD MATH

I understood vital mathematics before I learned good grammar.

Heroin + nostrils = deep nods.
Alcohol + oesophagus = fistfights.
Money + jewelry + new car = draggin' energy - gun = stupidity
Children - parents = misdirection
Innocent Black man + cop + racism + fear = hashtag
Hummingbirds + trenches = sacred songs
Percocet + Newport + pregnant woman = unforgotten miscarriage
Long day at work + $12 in pocket = Svedka
Payday = Grey Goose
Black man + stuntin' in a drop top Solara = his baby mother is at work
Designer bag + "new phone, who dis?" + new car = tax season

MARCH 11, 2017 AT 10:01 AM IN HAVANA, CUBA

To be honest, something inside of me doesn't wanna come back home. What if I just stay here? Enslaved tears broke themselves free today and slid down my cheeks. Today, suicidal thoughts broke bread with my body from the inside out—Am I her favorite dish? I receive calls from Heaven on the regular. I might pick up one of these days. I be lonely in a room full of people. I be feeling like old snow; everyone loved me when I arrived, but when they say how dark I could get, they stopped loving me. Every day, someone out there makes me feel bad for being Kondwani, as if I created this person. As if society had no parts. Giving all credit to the victim, instead of the victimizer. I'm living in a cave, and I'm a little paranoid. Not necessarily because of the cave, but the wind that seeps through the cracks. Will the wind carry me, or take me away? Every day, I'm living with raw wounds. Every day, I'm carving holes in the tunnel, hoping to find light in this dark tomb.
I just wanna get away.

Nonetheless, while I'm gone, just know that I'll be somewhere still writing my songs.

CHARLEENA LYLES

The sun dripped on my body like hot butter. You know, that summertime sun that drives children to swimming pools and emergency rooms. I stumbled out of North East Market, still drunk from the night before. I swallowed my chicken salad sandwich in five minutes tops, as if I haven't eaten in months. I opened my Twitter app and was punched dead in my face with a story headline: "Seattle police fatally shoot Black Seattle mother." I clicked the article, waiting for it to load, praying that it's clickbait. However, the mundane stories of cops killing Black people is something that's almost always true. I started reading, and my tear ducts became heavy like burdens. I discovered: a Black woman named Charleena Lyles called the police to report a burglary, and two cops pulled their triggers, murdering the 30-year-old pregnant-woman, in front of three children (ages 11, 4, and 1).

In these type of situations, I always ask myself, "Why couldn't the cop use a taser?" She was a small pregnant woman, surrounded by three kids, like c'mon? Then I remember, when police officers see Black skin, they black out and hunt for the smell of Black blood. Lives are taken all because a racist coward killer cop "feared for his/her life." Check this out: in America, it is acceptable for trained cops to panic and act on impulse, stripping someone's life. But, non-threatening and untrained citizens have to keep calm while cops poke pistols in their face. After seeing innocent Black people who mirror you get murdered by police, how can one keep calm when their life is up for grabs?

Situations like Charleena Lyles' and the countless others like hers, traumatize the family of the victims, and the bystanders who witness what happened. These devastating experiences also create a peculiar psyche in the minds of Black people. I can't help but think, "Will I be next?"

Charleena Lyles' family noted that she suffered from mental health issues. But wait, there's more. The Seattle Police Department has an ongoing federal consent decree, after a Department of Justice investigation found a pattern; officers engaging in excessive use of force, against people with mental or substance abuse problems. Therefore, Charleena was not the first Seattle Police Department's victim, and she will not be the last.

Tamir Rice was a child at a playground; Kathryn Johnson was 92-year-old woman, chilling in her own home; Philando Castile, whose murderer recently walked away with no convictions, was in the car with his girlfriend and child, and Charleena Lyles was pregnant. Racist institutions and killer cops DO NOT HAVE ANY PICKS. Any day, at any moment, your Black ass can be a hashtag, or a forgotten one. Your college degree, financial status, or your love for pumpkin spiced lattes cannot, and will not save you, if you are not white.

We are born into a world where there is a universal belief that is nourished in the minds of Americans: There is something wrong with Black people. By consuming this racist idea, when a Black person is MURDERED by a killer cop, people ask, "What did he/she do?" or some say, "It was a justified killing." In America, the word "justified" has racism scribbled all over it.

Hanging Black people by trees, dousing them in gasoline, setting their bodies in flames, cutting open pregnant bellies, and stampeding on the fetus—these were actions that were supported and sustained by America. And that's exactly why police can murder Blacks and don't get convicted; killer cops have replaced lynch mobs. The deaths of Sandra Bland, Korryn Gaines, Charleena Lyles, and the other unnamed Black women throughout history fit into the historical pattern of them committing the same crime: being a Black woman in America who resists white supremacy. And Black women who resist white supremacy are the biggest threats, because to a racist, Black women are scums of the Earth, and to murder the "loud mouth" ones is a means of social control. The murders that cops commit are warning shots to Black people in America. "Hey, this is what will happen to your Black ass if your rise up against white supremacy." Moral of the story.

Calling the police can cost you your life if you're Black. And at the rate that this country is going right now, you most definitely can be next, sooner than you think.

My heart goes out to every family member and friend of a victim who has been strangled to death by systemic oppression.

Let's continue to fight.

FREE SMOKE FOR THE PRESS

The government will break into homes
and put bullets in heads
over what was tweeted
Listen—It ain't just Twitter no more.

Facebook posts will get you clapped like an assembly
for spreading the real
Your writing will make a killing
Grandparents planning more funerals than Bingo nights
And, Mark Zuckerfuck ain't saving nobody.

Snapchat your chicken box
Location services on
and get snatched up and stored away
It's always been a death wish to tell the truth
You can't see what you saw.

Click the link in my bio   hazardous
Vulnerability on Instagram will have
them peoples pointing guns to ya
peephole, in an instance, fam.

Anybody can get it—you might be next
Them boys got Free Smoke for the Press.

Yo, when Dr. Ibram X. Kendi wrote, "When our reality is too ugly, we deny reality. It is too painful to look at. Reality is too hard to accept," I felt that…

I WANNA DIE YOUNG

"In this country a Black man only have like 5 years where he can exhibit maximum strength and that's right now while you're a teenager, while you're still strong, while you still wanna lift weights, while you still wanna shoot back. Cause once you turn 30 it's like they take the heart and soul out of a man, out of a Black man, in this country, and then you don't wanna fight no more."—2 Pac

I wanna die fighting. I wanna die young.

I don't wanna grow old. I don't want life to suck the marrow out of my bones how vampire bats inhale blood. Is that weird? I mean, the odds have to eventually win one day, right? I'm fine how I am now and I wanna die like this.

Growing up in Baltimore, I've seen the odds shoot first and ask questions later. I've seen the odds shatter Freddie Gray's voice box and smash his spinal cord. I've seen the odds kick down doorways and slam little unarmed babies to the ground because they looked "dangrous." I've seen the odds get shoved up Black nostrils—slow blinks until that last breath, yeah, that fentanyl is spine-chilling. I've seen the odds blast baseball-sized-bullet-holes through my homie Khalik's Honda coupe. I've seen the odds pick away at family trees like dollar scratch offs—Black bodies are dirt cheap in cities like mine. The odds forever win big around here.

A few years ago, three guys in Black hoodies rode through an East Baltimore neighborhood on small bicycles bangin' guns. Bullets stabbed my friend Darius's chest, which cracked open his 19-year-old heart. You're damn right he died.

Darius's death drove his brother Damon crazy, in the literal sense. To an outsider you would've thought the two were twins. They looked alike, shared the same smile, and it's rare that you caught one without the other. This was Damon's eleventh loved one that he lost by the time he turned 20. For the past few years, Damon has been in and out of psychiatric institutions; that large lump sum of friends he lost, and God knows whatever else he dealt with, has drove him crazy. I've seen it happen right before my eyes. The odds made the description of Damon change from "the coolest guy ever" to a guy "who wasn't always like that."

About a week ago I was riding passenger with my homie Pea (another close childhood friend) speeding through the streets of East Baltimore. I needed a seat belt, not as if I didn't have one on already. I needed another one because that's how loud his speakers were blastin' Lil Boosie's song "I Know." I saw Damon stumbling inside of a nearby liquor store, and I made Pea pull over so I could holla at him. He looked the same as he has for the past few years since the death of his brother. "Ayyeee Koni, that's really fucked up what they did to Darius, ain't it?" is how he starts off every convo. He then repeatedly says his brother's name, head trembling, while dry crust and drool hangs out the corner of his 22-inch rim-sized-mouth. Damon's body odor used to smell like expensive cologne—it's been replaced with the stench of cigarette smoke, the cheapest liquor on the planet, rotten eggs, and dead rats. As Damon stumbled away and I walked back towards Pea's car, I heard people from the neighborhood whisper, "Mmmm, that boy wasn't always like that," a phrase that I frequently say to myself i a lot in reference to Damon. I've seen him transform from a happy, loving, big brother and son, who's always cracking jokes, to a crazed drunk. Damon has been fighting the odds since he peeked his chocolate-rello-colored eyes out of his mother's vagina, just like the others who grew up in poverty. Some beat the odds, but the majority of the time, people don't.

I've seen several friends and associates fade into a foreign mental state. I know so many young women and men who "weren't always like that." When you know that African-Americans who live below the poverty line experience extreme psychological distress, then you cannot help but to see why many Black people die young, or wanna die young.

I've seen the odds slurp up vulnerable bodies, break their bones using its tongue, then spit out the remainders into that dark hole that "life's troubles" carves out for its victims. I guess the bright side to entering this dark place is that you'll never be alone.

The odds have back-to-back triple doubles around here. Around here, the odds score all net. The odds perform no-look-alley-oops around here.

That's why I wanna die young. I don't want the odds to even think twice that it'll do me like the rest of them. I don't want my future to get straightjacketed by the odds.

I wanna die like this.

I wanna die 5'9–152 lbs—with a loud mouth—unapologetic and filled with energy on my worst days—humble—writing and saying whatever I want, when I want, how I want—lion-hearted, and turnt. I wanna die turnt.

I don't want the odds to bury me alive. I wanna die who I am right now. I wanna die young.

HOW-TO-HIDE

I provide the liquor
a few jokes, ideas, and new music
You provide me comfort
A body to hold onto long enough
until it's time for me to dip.
Again, finding something new
I was raised to be a runner baby
I've been running all my life
Away, but I realized there is no such place
But still, I continue to run.

JUNE 3, 2018 AT 7:11 AM IN BALTIMORE

Poems aren't an opportunity to show how smart you are.
Poetry is what you feel. What makes you laugh? What makes
you cry? What's beautiful? What's ugly?—Answer those
questions, and that is poetry.

I AM THANKFUL FOR MY GRANDMOTHER

A sickness kicked my mother in the belly in 1992 while she was getting her hair done by her friend Tina. My mother walked to Johns Hopkins Hospital, got seen, and found out that she was pregnant. The wind danced around my mother as she marched her pudgy belly down Monument Street, heading back home. Although my mother was now eating for two, she didn't bother to change her unhealthy eating or drug habits. For nine months I kicked, screamed, cried, and gagged in a cocaine and heroin-wrapped placenta. My life was non-existence way before my sugar brown eyes kissed the sunlight.

On June 3, 1993, my mother gave birth to an "at-risk" youth. My mother couldn't stay sober long enough to get a job, let a lone raise a child. Around the time of my birth, my grandmother had just been offered a job promotion that she later declined. Not only did she decline the promotion, but she quit her job and started a career as a daycare provider. That way, she could keep the cash flowing, and she could work out of her home to take care of me, my mother, and the other children who came later.

I hit many stumbling blocks growing up: selling heroin and

cocaine to my friends' parents and grandparents, joining a gang and being Blood affiliated, and getting arrested—all before I hit the 9th grade. However, I have many friends who had it worse growing up.

In Baltimore, it is almost impossible for young people to grow up in the city and not indulge in "trouble." Trouble whispers. Trouble screams. Trouble becomes your best friend. Trouble becomes your enemy. No matter what trouble is disguised in, you will have a date with her, one day, while living and dying under Baltimore's skies.

Despite the issues I faced growing up--abandonment, child neglect, mental abuse, and the trauma of losing friends and family to murder and prison cells--I've had so many friends who struggled much more than I did, while having less. Less food in the pantry. Less love behind the peephole. Fewer clothes in the closet.

Some of my friends were raised by both parents and some weren't. Most of the time their parents were present physically, but not spiritually and emotionally; therefore, they were absent, leaving my friends to raise themselves.

I live in a city where children take care of themselves, then get enough money and enough age to take care of their parents and grandparents.

My grandmother played an important role in my life and always made sure that I had the basic needs. I've never starved, like many of my friends. I've never had to jam pistols to skulls in return for money, like many of friends. I've never been homeless, sleeping in the cold rain, like many of my friends. I've never had to drop out of school to be "the man of the house," at age 14, like many of my friends.

If it wasn't for my grandmother I would've been living and dying, like many of my friends. In many Black communities grandmothers have always been the backbone of the family, and the community.

Whatever I end up calling this piece; a letter, a song, or a poem, it is to give thanks to my grandmother. If it wasn't for the love she had for my mother and her unborn son in the early 90's, I would not be the person I am today.

Always remember to be thankful for what you have because someone else out there has less.

Down Da Hill

Lead paint chips, Flaming Hot Cheetos, broken liquor bottles, empty valves, vacant homes, the smell of rotten breath begging for cash, churches filled with a bunch of broke Niggas. The pastor pushes Porsche pedals and his members stack pennies cause they spent their hard earned dollars, on hope Nigga. Granny attempted to block demons with toys, testaments, and tambourines.

But, trauma rolls 10 deep. Trauma tip-tocs. No, trauma sprints. No, trauma stomps

NOVEMBER 13, 2017 AT 1:48 PM IN GEORGETOWN,
WASHINGTON, D.C.,

Grandma used to spank my bare Black ass until it turned
plum, the same shade of the wine she used to drank—for not
snatching the chicken out of the freezer to unthaw, two hours
ago. This made everyone in the family tummies roar
for an extra hour or so.

RINGLING FOES

"Ringling Bros. Circus Closing After 146 Years"

I saw this and sarcastically said to myself, "Oh no! Not 'The Greatest Show on Earth.'"

Top articles covered: the 146 years of "greatness"; the mistreatment, abuse and murder of exotic animals, which led to battles with animal-rights groups; and the too-little, too-late attempt to hire its first African-American ringmaster. However, none of the articles identified how P.T. Barnum's rise to fame in the 19th century should be credited to his exploitation of African Americans. Harriet Washington's Medical Apartheid revealed that in 1835 in New York City, Barnum debuted Joice Heth, an African-American slave woman, at his first show, which was titled, "Greatest Natural and National Curiosity in the World." Barnum claimed that Heth was a 161-year-old blind woman who had nursed George Washington.

This blind, sickly woman racked up massive coins for Barnum. When she died the following year, Barnum immediately paid a surgeon to publicly dissect Heth among 1,500 spectators. This was without her consent. He turned her autopsy procedure into a spectacle, profiting by charging 50 cents a person.

Years after Heth's death, the demand for "Negro freaks" soared. Barnum shows now included conjoined twins and people who suffered from elephantiasis, vitiligo, blindness and other anomalies, all of whom were Black. Barnum was not only creating entertainment for white racists but was also perpetuating the idea of the medical racial inferiority of Black people. This prejudice was already deeply ingrained as part of the medical scene, especially in the South.

"We need P.T. Barnum, a little bit, because we have to build up the image of our country." — President Donald Trump

Not only did Barnum exploit Black people who had birth defects, but some of his "acts" were surgically impaired to fit falsified life stories. By desecrating Black bodies for grotesque amusement, he opened the door for racist physicians and scientists to experiment on and torture Black people all over the world.

Barnum perpetuated the idea of Black people as freaks, hypersexual beasts and illiterates by publicly displaying crippled, physically disabled and half-naked images of them for his circus acts. Barnum was no different from the doctors who were involved in the Tuskegee syphilis experiment; no different from Thomas Jefferson, who injected his slaves with smallpox; and no different from the hundreds of poor Black people whom Johns Hopkins Hospital exploited for immoral experimentation. I grew up in a neighborhood an arm's length away from Johns Hopkins, and I have family and friends who were made mentally, financially and intellectually inferior from undergoing unethical procedures.

P.T. Barnum, and other idiotic racists, believed that Black people were (and still are) naturally illiterate, experimental animals; disease-ridden, lazy, cursed children of Ham; and people who could withstand more pain than whites. These false ideas about Black people justified the enslavement, medical torture and murder of Black people in this country.

If the gatekeepers of white supremacy could drop bombs on every impoverished Black neighborhood in the U.S., they would. But they can't because we live in a society where money matters, and Black dollars hold more value than Black lives. Black people will continue to be subjected to crummy health care, along with other racist ideas and policies, to ensure their degradation. This will only come to a stop if people view and treat one another as human beings.

Ever since slavery was "abolished," America has continued to replace one form of slavery with another, systematically keeping a majority of the Black population padlocked to poverty, prisons, health defects and graveyards. We continually blame the Black struggle in America on Black people, and not on the system that has enslaved, murdered and oppressed Black people, and continues to do so. The ending of the Barnum reign is even more peculiar because President Donald Trump believes that the country needs someone like Barnum.

In January 2016, Trump appeared on Meet the Press. Chuck Todd asked Trump, "What's any of those do you consider a compliment?" referring to the names people had call him. Trump responded, "P.T. Barnum." His explanation followed:

"We need P.T. Barnum, a little bit, because we have to build up the image of our country." From the beginning, this system has beaten down "ugly" Black people to "build up the image of our country," which is synonymous with building up white supremacy and maintaining Black inferiority.

I say with great delight, so long to the worst show on Earth.

GOD TALK

Rappers are Gods in my community.

The lines that they scribble move moons
The verses that they rap make you abuse
rewind buttons
Genius literature that we call, bars.

Good records are revolution wrapped in plastic
Hip hop breaks ankles, do no look passes
toss alley oops, and dunk backwards.

Rappers are Gods in my community.

JUNE 10, 2018 AT 5:32 PM IN BALTIMORE

We have to stop blaming "God's design" on the work of man.

EDUCATION BEHIND THE BARS OF POVERTY: CONDITIONS OF LEARNING ENVIRONMENTS IN BALTIMORE AND BEYOND

"The future of the negro lies more in the research laboratory than in the schools...when diseased, he should be registered and forced to take treatment before he offers his diseased mind and body on the altar of academic and professional education"
- Thomas Murrell, M.D., U.S. Public Health Service, 1910; Medical Apartheid

Baltimore City students have been getting pistol whipped and robbed of their education for many years. Baltimore is currently trending in the media due to the ice-box-conditions in some of the public schools—some thermostats read 30+ degrees.

Pictures of injustice made a lighting attack across the internet—snapshots of Baltimore students wearing gloves, coats, and hats, and pictures of the damage caused by broken boilers and bursting pipes. A similar story emerged in September of 2017 when classrooms inside of Patterson High School reached over 100 degrees for consecutive days, where students sweat bullets attempting to learn while being smothered in Satan's arms. The system's chief operations officer Keith Scroggins had said, "We are doing everything we can to install air conditioning in our schools to make them more comfortable." and with "limited funding, the process is expected to take five years."

Baltimore is the largest city in the richest state in the U.S. and our children are forced to sit in these horrific conditions disguised as schools, and the excuse is "limited funding."

This might be someone's first time hearing about students being forced to flirt with death inside of public schools, however, America has maintained racial inequalities in education for many years.

On April 12, 1860, The Mississippi Senator, who later became president, Jefferson Davis, delivered a speech objecting a bill funding education in Washington D.C. In his speech he stated, "This government was not founded by negroes nor for negroes but by white men for white men...the inequality of the white and Black races was 'stamped from the beginning.'" Davis, along with many other racists in this country, have and still currently believe that Black people are biologically distinct from and inferior to white people. Therefore, handing something over as powerful as education to a group of subhuman Black monsters would be blasphemous, and it would debunk their beloved white supremacy.

November 1, 1864 was Maryland's Emancipation Day. In the book Stamped From The Beginning, Dr. Ibram X. Kendi wrote that the newly-free people flashed and paraded to the President's house where Lincoln gave a speech and encouraged them to improve their moral character and intellectual capacity. Lincoln said this, but supported Maryland's constitution, which didn't allow Blacks to vote or attend public schools. Lincoln expected newly-free Blacks to two-step into freedom without a stumble after being desecrated by slavery. That is the same ideology that people have when they expect students in Baltimore public schools to receive a quality education in heinous environments—only to blame the children, and not the school system that enslaves, oppresses, and mis-educates the children of color.

I've spoke at several schools in Maryland, from suburban to urban, from majority Black to majority white schools. The suburban and majority white schools have floors clean enough to eat off of and are equipped with state of the art technology. When I'm in the urban and majority Black schools I can't decipher whether the schools look like prisons, or the prisons look like these schools. The students read from ancient textbooks with missing pages, sit at the same desk that our great-grandparents sat, and are being taught on 100 year old chalkboards.

In early 2017, The Baltimore Sun released an article that stated, "In the seven years since the first of Maryland's six casinos opened, they have pumped $1.7 billion into the state's Education Trust Fun." The audacious claim that the state has "limited funding" is an insult to the people of Baltimore. Using the term "limited funding" is an escape to avoid providing a legitimate educational environment for Baltimore City students, forcing them to suffer in cruel conditions. Being as though it is politically incorrect for racists to use the "N-word" and call us biologically inferior, they swap it out with terms that drip with racism, such as "limited funding."

When talking about "low test scores" or "disruptive Black

students," the basic resources that these children lack always gets left out of the narrative. The state of Maryland opened a $35 million youth detention facility in Baltimore, but officials say that it'll take up to five years for the city schools to have something as basic as air and heat. This sends a message to the entire Black community—the U.S. government is more focused on padlocking Black youth to prison cells, as opposed to giving them valuable education. We don't need anyone to say, "America doesn't care about Black people," when actions—or lack thereof—speak volumes.

Black people in Baltimore have a long history of taking matters into their own hands when systemic oppression pops off its face mask. It brought me immense joy to see Samierra Jones, a senior at Coppin State University start a GoFundMe and raise over $40,000 with the help of a few other Baltimoreans—one of them being Aaron Maybin who teaches at Matthew A. Henson. This caught the eye of many celebrities, including Chris Brown, who shared the GoFundMe to his 41.4 million Instagram followers. The money that's been raised will be used to purchase roughly 600 space heaters and winter outerwear for Baltimore City students.

There is a rotten myth that says in order for Black people to have a fair shot in the country, new laws need to be passed. To those who believe that, I say this: If the government isn't currently enforcing the laws that are supposed to provide Black people equality and protection from racism, why do you think they will enforce additional laws? America is morally obligated to find new and creative ways to exclude Black people from laws that are said to be in their favor.

In oppressed communities, real change always happens on the

ground level. In fact, Huey Newton once said "The revolution has always been in the hands of the young. The young always inherit the revolution." Seeing the progress that Samierra and other fellow Baltimore residents have made in a short amount of hours to help aid our students during this icy-crisis shows me that there is hope in my city. The kind of love that Black people have for one another during tough times is unmatched, euphoric, and revolutionary. In America, Black people are born into legally binding relationships where they get enslaved, tortured, and oppressed on various levels. On each of these levels it calls for individuals who are willing to fight and to share resources and skills to people who aren't afforded them. For example, I play my role by devoting much of my time to teaching students the importance of literacy and storytelling which gets them excited about reading and sharing their own stories. Getting students to understand the importance of these things will grant them critical thinking skills, and with those skills, I believe it can help them maneuver more efficiently through systemic oppression. There is an ongoing war between the education system and Black communities, and it is a war we're going to ride out together.

WHERE MY HUG AT?

Don't fall in love
with the block
it won't blow you a kiss back,
till death
it will hug you until your rib cage crushes.

(I wrote this on a napkin and I can't remember what day and time it was. I know that it was early 2018 and it was snowing hard as hell outside)

I was sitting in Moby Dick House of Kabob on West 40th street in Baltimore. While I waited for my food, there was a small child running around the restaurant. It looked like he was having the time of his life. This random old guy looked over to me and said, "Kids are beautiful, aren't they? Kids are God's angels until we turn em into the devils that we are."

BALTIMORE CEASEFIRE

There isn't a corner in my city that hasn't been disturbed by violence. I've routinely lost friends and family to it since I was a child. It will forever and always be present in this country, especially in impoverished communities.

There is no one-sized-fit all solution to stop the violence, but, there is a radical and ground-breaking movement happening in Baltimore to slow it down and revitalize how people cope with the trauma. PTSD is an unsung tune in our community, but it inflicts mental instabilities on the thousands of people in the aftershock of their loved ones being killed.

I didn't think so when I first heard about it, but Baltimore Ceasefire 365 is the guardian angel that my city needs.

The goal is for people around the city to engage in life-affirming activities, along with putting a muzzle on violence in the community. The first ceasefire was took place the first weekend in August last year and there was no murder for a total of 67 out of the 72 hours. This was still ground-breaking as statistics proved – at this time there was one murder every nineteen hours. The second ceasefire, which took place in three months later in November saw art installations, workshops and a community tailgate, but was marred by a murder 26 hours in.

The third quarterly Ceasefire took place February 2018, with a packed programme of community events, including people were leaving visible markers in the places where people have been killed. They're turning what were once murder scenes into sacred places.

Baltimore Ceasefire 365 was founded by Erricka Bridgeford with an organizing committee of five men and women from across the Baltimore community. Mrs. Bridgeford's own harrowing journey is behind the idea: murder snatched two of her cousins, a brother, and a step son.

"Every time there's a ceasefire weekend and someone gets killed, we immediately find that family and give them money," explains Bridgeford. Funds are donated and she goes to explain that the money can be used for anything from funeral expenses, to fresh sneakers: noting that healing mechanisms are subjective and that they want what's best for everyone.

In the process of hitting the streets, Ms Bridgeford and other organizers ask the people of the community "What do you need in your life that will help make things better for you and your loved ones?" The idea is to be hands-on, sharing resources that can help people struggling with legal issues, financial trouble and mental health issues.

The Baltimore Ceasefire is geared not only towards stopping shootings, but all violence. I spoke with Hannah Brancato, who's a part of the Monument Quilt Project who held a workshop during the ceasefire to honour victims of domestic homicide. On the quilt were collections of stories from people who've been impacted by rape and abuse, along with messages of support from others.

I asked Brancato her thoughts on the importance of practicing art in communities—and specifically the way in which yoga and fitness being practiced in urban communities to help heal the people. Hannah responded, "Envisioning the world we want to live in, and dreaming about something different is necessary for social change work—and for our own well-being. In that way, we can be free and help each other get free."

As I scanned the room I saw Bridgeford's mother, who was sitting with her 18-year-old granddaughter. I asked them about generational trauma, since all three of them are engaged in working on a solution. Bridgeford's mother saw domestic violence as a child, but believes the cycle stopped because she was able to limit what her children would and would not see. It was these principles which her daughter would carry forward when raising her own children.

Much like Bridgeford and her family, I believe that if we can pass down trauma from generation to generation, we can do the same with healing and nurturing, forming new foundations of love. Baltimore Ceasefire 365 is showing us the way.

2-WEEKS-NOTICE

Slaving half past dead
My time, I've done
My dues, I paid em
Right now I want out
Don't question me
Before you say a word
Yes, I do wanna go through with this

I wanna be free
Free like Robin
like Kate
Free like Simone
Free like…

God
Why you play so much?
Should've been phoned me home

I wish that life was like the work place.
Put in your two weeks and call it quits
Without being judged by your family and peers.

I did my time
I paid my dues
I kept it cool

Now, I just want out.

JULY 11, 2018 AT 12:45 PM IN BALTIMORE

How many fights does a boy have to fight,
till he becomes a man?

SUPERWOMAN

"One of the most awkward conversations is when I tell people I have cancer," says Tiarnee Yates.

Tiarnee calls it "the three reactions": 1. He or she has an awkward, silent stare. 2. He or she asks billions of questions. And 3. He or she says, "You don't look like you have cancer."

For Tiarnee, age 23, her ongoing struggle with cancer began during a basketball tournament in March of 2008. She was dominating—until the fifth game of the day when the then-13-year-old's heart became a clenched fist and breathing became difficult.

Her team, the Baltimore Storm, lost that game and many people, including Tiarnee's father, were upset about the loss and said she blew the game due to "laziness." A few days later before practice, Tiarnee began wheezing heavily while walking up a flight of stairs. She didn't know what was wrong and her wheezing kept getting worse.

Her mother carried her into GBMC's emergency room but those "laziness" accusations stayed with her, so Tiarnee said,

"Ma, we need to hurry up and get this over with, I gotta get to practice."

X-rays followed and Tiarnee was quickly transported to Johns Hopkins Hospital: Her "laziness" turned out to be a broken piece of her kidney, cemented between her heart and lungs. She convinced herself nothing severe was going on; her biggest concerns were missing school and prepping for a championship game. That night, Tiarnee went to sleep worried but determined, only to wake up to 15 or so friends and family members looming, almost smothering her with concern.

"I must be dying," she recalls thinking as she spotted her grandmother's face and realized she'd made the trip from Virginia to Baltimore to see her granddaughter.

Cat scans, more X-rays, nurses, needles, blood, and thoughts of death swarmed Tiarnee for a month and a half as she stayed at the hospital. At one point, Tiarnee flatlined. Friends and family scattered as a team of doctors and nurses assembled, rushed her to another room, where she was examined with another scan.

Tiarnee was still focused on practice and when a doctor entered the room to tell her some news she assumed meant all was well.

"I can go back to school?" she asked preemptively. "I'm pretty sure they told you that I've been missing practice."

"You're gonna be out a little bit longer than expected. You have cancer," the doctor told her.

Tiarnee was diagnosed with renal cell carcinoma, a rare kidney cancer.

"Y'all are bullshittin', I have basketball to finish," Tiarnee said.

"You might not be able to play basketball for a while," the doctor told her.

About three weeks after that game she lost to laziness, Tiarnee received her first surgery, which removed the blockage between her heart and lung and removed her right kidney. Her doctors predicted Tiarnee would be dead very soon, maybe even shortly after her surgery.

While she recovered, basketball stayed on her mind. One night she woke up in the hospital to her father watching a basketball game, and promptly yelled "What's the score?"

For the next two months, she stayed in the hospital with doctors running in and out of her room to check in on her. She says she felt as if she was in "a freak show."

But Tiarnee recovered quickly and was released from the hospital. She went back to school in May and graduated from Cardinal Shehan Middle School that June. She attended Polytechnic High School and was frequently bullied for the face mask that she wore along with her uniform—due to her fragile immune system.

"I don't ever want anybody to feel pity for me," she says.

Tiarnee keeps a sense of humor about it all—renal cell carcinoma is typically found in men in the age range of 60 and up, and for a young woman to get this type of cancer is rare, so she sarcastically calls herself "The Lucky One." She is frank about her experience with chemotherapy.

"I was ignorant [of chemotherapy]; I heard so much bad stuff about chemo: It kills people. You go bald," she says. "I wasn't worried about dying. I was worried about losing my hair. I thought to myself 'Oh my god, my edges are gonna be gone.'"

Tiarnee went through chemotherapy every Thursday all through high school. She lost weight, hair, and even friends. She bitterly recalls people attempting to do things for her such as take her out on dates or to the prom because they felt sorry for her.

After graduating high school in 2012, Tiarnee attended Saint Peters University in Jersey City and received her bachelors degree in science and health with a concentration in physical therapy in May 2016.

At times, however, anxiety and depression and the trauma of recovery haunt her. She missed what added up to over two years of high school and college during recovery due to numerous appointments and six surgeries. A September 2015 surgery to remove cancer from her liver was her "worst surgery ever." It was so spiritually, mentally, and physically damaging that she considered suicide by overdosing on prescription pills. During her recovery of this surgery, she says her grandmother told her, "It's not your turn yet."

Despite the many times Tiarnee has been plugged up to machines, unable to walk, breathe, or talk, plagued by suicidal thoughts, she has persevered. It's the same spirit that had her fighting her mom on the way to the hospital and the one that told her doctor they were "bullshittin'" and she had a game to play.

I consider Tiarnee my superhero, and whenever I start bitching and moaning, I always think about Tiarnee and what she's faced and gulp down my cries. She is now pursuing a Masters in Sports and Fitness at Winthrop University in South Carolina.

Although Tiarnee can no longer run basketball plays such as "Trap Girl," drain three pointers, celebrate victories, and embrace the losses, she has found other ways to engage with world. Along with her academic studies, Tiarnee hopes to raise money for research to help other cancer patients and intends to start her own program that encourages and assists men and women who suffer from cancer to "stay beautiful" despite the hardships they are facing. She's already looking for donations of new clothes, shoes, and wigs for the participants in the program.

Her head may be bloody, but it's unbowed.

When I finally asked Tiarnee if she fears death, she erupted with a "Hell no!" Then she goes on.

"But I do look at the world differently because I was supposed to die at 13," she says. "I'm not going anywhere no time soon. I will never say 'cancer beat me.' I can't leave even if I wanted to because if I quit, it's gonna affect people in a negative way and make others want to quit."

TIARNEE'S SONG

You sit consecutively at the number one spot
A quadruple platinum record with no features
Party over, I go home and leave you on repeat

You post a picture on the gram, I go ape shit
I go nuts, I be geekin off you, I be trippin
Oh, I text that shit to all of my friends.
I save that shit…you all up in my archives

Your draggin' energy unmatched
Sexless, still
Not doing it, exciting
A love supreme
Hot horns blow
itching for a fan
and I'm your number 1 Stan
Ya sharpest shooter

But, take ya time when you liking a guy
cause if he sense that your feelings too intense,
it's drip or die

I promise that I'll always sing about you.

MARCH 22, 2018 AT 4:11 AM IN STRATFORD, LONDON

The social construct that kills humans who lack thereof. And in the same breath, the same social construct that reveals artistry in the caterpillar, before it transforms into a butterfly. If it even lives that long. Beauty. Beauty, never really dies.

UNO

Me: "Haha! draw 4!"

Love: "No, you draw 4. Skip you, back to me. Skip you, back to me. Reverse, back to me, reverse back to me. Uno. Uno out!"

Me: "Damn, that's how you feel?"

Love: Why you so mad bruh? It's nothing personal. it's just a game.

JUNE 10, 2018 AT 6:08 PM IN BALTIMORE

Every time I feel a hint of emptiness, I fill it with hope.

WATER OF LIFE

We drink we fuck
We laugh we cry
We love we trip
No bags we sky

We place the pain
Right there aside
Them Bible rules
We don't abide

We live our lives
We think we do
We walk for miles
In concrete shoes

We only do
What we are taught
Our livers bad
We lit—a sport

We eat, repeat

We drink more vodka
than water these days.

MY FIRST WHIP

I hopped in my 1995 Monte Carlo—a green 2 door Z34
I was a teenager, left hand on the wheel while my right
was busy with a red cup running over with Ciroc.

I crushed the pedal and guess what?
Potholes punished my tires.

My check engine light was smiling
brighter than a boy who just smelled
his first vagina.
My oil had a jheri curl drip.
My breaks screamed every time my shoe tapped.
My AC was college kid broke.

I arrived at my destination
and the girl I intended to see
did not respond to my text.

Her name was Angel,
but she ain't have Heaven's scent.
She left me hanging
like teardrops on a chin.
This was supposed to be our first date.

Months later, still nothing.
Not even a "Hey, sorry for what happened."

Broken promises from a broken bird.

She said it was undeniable that she would
change my life.

The only thing that changed was how I viewed her.

I thought she would help me become free.
I left the trenches and realized
college was a girl that ain't cracked
up to what she's supposed to be.

ACKNOWLEDGEMENTS

Thank you God for giving me the breath to share my gifts with the world. I want to also thank both of my grandmothers for the sacrifices that you made to help create a better life for me growing up in Baltimore. Last but not least, thanks to all of my family and friends for the undying support and love that you have demonstrated over the years.

Make sure you pursue your passion today.

PHOTO BY GORDON MENSAH

KONDWANI FIDEL

ABOUT THE AUTHOR

Kondwani Fidel is a poet and essayist that has toured in the United Kingdom and lectured and taught classes at the University of East London. He has also lectured and shared poetry at countless universities, conferences, and literary events across America.

Fidel has been featured in *Washington Post, Mic, CNN,* and elsewhere, and has made television appearances on *RT America.* He has been published in *The Root, The Afro,* and *City Paper. The Baltimore Sun* honored Fidel in the 2018 issue of 'Best of Baltimore', as a change maker who is working to improve the Baltimore area with his courage, innovative thinking, and leadership.

Fidel is a M.F.A. Candidate at the University of Baltimore, concentrating on Creative Writing and Publishing Arts. He is from, and currently lives in, Baltimore, Maryland.

He is also the author of *Raw Wounds,* and the founder of 'READ' (a clothing company that's mission is to promote the importance of literacy)

www.KondwaniFidel.com
Instagram & Twitter: @KondwaniFidel
Facebook: www.facebook.com/KondwaniFidel
Email: Kondwani@KondwaniFidel.com

Made in the USA
Middletown, DE
05 August 2018